NATE HOLDRIDGE

Dear New Dad

By Nate W. Holdridge

Copyright © 2013 by Calvary Monterey

ISBN-10: 1493646540
ISBN-13: 978-1493646548

Printed in the United States of America.

Table of Contents

Introduction

A LETTER

Dear New Dad,

I am incredibly excited for you. To be a father has been one of the greatest joys of my life. I have thoroughly enjoyed leading and teaching my children. I am watching God grow my life through my relationship with my three daughters. Whenever I meet a man who is about to become a father for the first time, I rejoice with strong anticipation of the great experiences about to unfold in his life. Whenever I come across a father of young children, I smile at the possibilities of love, adventure, and leadership that await him. The potential joys and agonies, the highs and lows of fatherhood are grand.

I am also incredibly terrified for you. The responsibilities of parents are immense, but the great responsibility of a father knows no bounds. The massive influence we will have in the lives of our children is staggering. To look into their little eyes and see their expectation and need is truly humbling. To realize, in the midst of all of it, that you are the man for the job can be an altogether overwhelming realization.

Fortunately, there is great and wonderful hope in Jesus Christ. The God who was able to redeem a broken mess of a world is able to mend our personal brokenness and prepare us to be the men and fathers He has called us to be. As fathers, our influence can be used for incredible good by the power of the Holy Spirit living in and through us. These precious and new little lives God has entrusted into our care can grow into up into maturity, ever thankful for the dad God has given to them. There is great hope.

As you read this little book, there are a few things I'd like you to know from the outset. Firstly, while this is an intentionally short book (it is a book for new dads, after all), it is also a dense book. Each role observed on these pages could be exhausted with many more chapters, books, and thoughts. For this reason, I encourage you to give the Holy Spirit time and space to talk to your heart directly about each one of these roles. Go slowly, write down potential thoughts, and allow God to do a work in your heart.

Secondly, I'd like you to know that this is a "gospel-required" kind of book. There might be a few good moral principles and fatherly tricks and tips to glean from the pages found here, but this book will be most valuable to those who have placed their faith in the substitutionary death of Jesus Christ, believing upon His resurrection and trusting His Word completely.

Thirdly, I want you to know how hard I try to preach these messages to myself. I rejoice at what God has done in my life, but I am not a perfect man who has already arrived. As you read these pages, understand that the author has allowed and will allow these truths to continue to wash over him. Perhaps this will be helpful for you to know.

Lastly—and this should go without saying—please know that only God's perfect Word is without error and flaw. Any and every book on parenting will miss the mark here or there, perhaps sharing thoughts and perspectives that are valuable in one setting or scenario yet not in another. I'm sure you already had this mind-set, but I thought I'd throw it out there to cover my bases. I'm just another dude.

I wish you well and, in a general sense, am praying for you as you embark on this short Scriptural journey. I hope the Bible comes more alive inside of your heart as you apply it to the tremendous challenge and privilege of fatherhood. I believe in you, but more importantly, the Lord believes in you because He *"is able to do far more abundantly than all that we ask or think, according to the power at work within us..."* (Ephesians 3:20). God bless you. Go get it. You can nail this.

In Christ,
Nate Holdridge

Chapter 1

SON

And he said to them, "When you pray, say: 'Father...'" (Luke 11:2)

Recently, on a Sunday morning, a time when I am usually thoroughly engaged in teaching, preaching, and personal ministry, I found a quiet moment to observe and reflect on the people God has entrusted into our pastoral care. As I sat and watched, I saw laughter and friendship, pain and endurance, joy and challenge. I saw generations on the move, generations desiring to honor Christ with their lives. And I saw pregnant women. Lots of them. I thought to myself, "Someone did that to them. If I can, I would love to help those fathers."

Over the ages various tides of thought and influence have churned throughout the world, but some realities remain constant. One of those constants is the importance of the role of the father in the family and society. While a male will contribute to a pregnancy, a father contributes to a legacy. Every person on earth is shaped in some way by his or her father. Like the church, family is an entity created and designed by God, and fathers play a huge role in the development and leadership of the individual family.

Unfortunately, the definition of what a father even is has come under much duress in recent years. The role is seen by some as dispensable, redundant, and occupied by the moronic. Dads are needled and ridiculed in pop culture as mindless numbskulls with misogynistic tendencies. Needless to say, God's view of the role is a high one, evidenced by the fact it is a title He reserves for Himself. He calls Himself our Father. All who are covered by the blood of Christ have a Father in the God of Heaven.

I know many families will be forced to adapt themselves to something other than the father-and-mother-and-children-living-under-one-roof paradigm. Sometimes this is simply the result of sin in general, the basic brokenness of the world, causing the death of parents through some catastrophe or sickness. At other times this is the result of personal sin, such as when a man decides to abandon a woman he impregnated or divorce a woman he married to pursue other things. I hope for this short book to be of help to every family, whatever its condition. Still, recognizing all of this, my aim will be to hold out the ideal structure, trusting the Holy Spirit to help everyone in less-than-ideal situations to find the glimmers of light and hope and adaptions they need as they attempt to apply the wonderful truth of God's Word.

Now, back to those new dads I mentioned. I know firsthand how overwhelming, exciting, nerve-racking, and pressure filled those first years of fathering can be. I congratulate you on beginning this journey, whether you planned on it or not! The reality is that this role is one of the most important roles you will ever fill, one of the most world-changing and generation-shaping responsibilities you will ever carry, a task that will likely leave its mark on the earth well after you are dead and gone.

Most of us want to do it right. We want to be a blessing. We long for the areas of influence God has given to us to be better off as a result of our being there (see 2 Corinthians 10:13–16 for Paul's area of influence). Sadly, however, we often lack the simple tools needed to get the job done. Poor models, misperceptions regarding our role, or our own lethargy can distract us from the great task at hand. I pray this little read will help you in some way to find some of the tools you need to get the job done right and to get started on the right foot.

Your Father in Heaven

The funny thing about fathering is that even though the influence is so great and the responsibility so intense, billions of us have done it. Some have fathered well and some have fathered poorly, but it isn't exactly a role you go to school for. There is no small segment of professional fathers for the rest of us amateurs to look up to. No, we all have to figure it out and learn and grow as this role in life comes our way.

If there ever was a professional father, it would have to be God Himself. He is the ultimate Father. He defines. He protects. He teaches. He leads. He loves. He delights in His children. He gives an identity and a heritage to all who become His own.

One of the strongest words I could give to you is the encouragement to experience God as your Heavenly Father. This comes first by placing your faith and trust in the work of Jesus on the cross in dying substitutionally for your sin and rising from the dead. Secondly, however, this comes through a practical and experiential relationship with the God of heaven, a relationship made possible exclusively by the blood of Jesus. Day by day, week by week, and year by year, as you experience the wonderful fathering ministry of God, you will become strengthened as a man to become a greater father than you ever would be in your own natural ability. Over time, his nature will change and transform you (see 2 Corinthians 3:18). You will always become more like the God you worship.

The Lord delights in you as His child. He longs to serve you and care for you personally. *"The Lord reproves him whom he loves, as a father the son in whom he delights"* (Proverbs 3:12). Perhaps for you, up to this time, a relationship with God, called by some a walk with God, has been a foreign concept. Perhaps you are yet to discover the joy of receiving direction, correction, and identification from your Father in heaven. If there was ever a time to get on that bus, it's when a man begins a family.

Your family needs you to begin interacting with your Father in heaven like crazy right now. They need you to press in. This can be an extremely difficult thing to do once a baby comes into your life. When my second daughter was born, it felt like she didn't sleep for two years. My poor wife was extremely worn out. I was very fatigued. Time with God was extremely hard to come by during that season, but every time I fought for it I found it to be greatly rewarding (see Hebrews 11:6). A little time in His Word always went such a long way toward directing me and speaking into my heart. Often in His Word I would find the encouragement, correction, or perspective I needed for that particular day. Like the manna falling daily from heaven in the Old Testament era, my Father in heaven fed me spiritually on a daily basis.

No, this is not the time to shelve your walk with God. This is a time to pick up the pace. Your children need a godly man, a man focused on the priorities and thoughts of God. Your wife needs a spiritual man, a man who is doing everything he can to crush his sinful tendencies and become a servant to his bride. It is good and wonderful to learn of the *practicalities* of being a father here on earth, but it is of extreme importance to *practice your relationship* with your Father in heaven. Place your relationship with Him at the center of everything you are. Don't allow your walk with Him to be just one part of who you are, but all of who you are. He must color and influence every other part of your life. Don't be deceived into thinking this isn't an important part of your role as a father. Without a strong relationship with your Heavenly Father you won't have the strength to provide all that is needed for your family.

Scripture

Your word is a lamp to my feet and a light to my path. (Psalms 119:105)

Allow the Word of God to saturate your mind as a new or expecting father. Sit under Bible teaching, read the Word of God for personal learning and growth, and write down various truths that have become meaningful to you as you study and read. Each day, even if only briefly, give God permission to speak into your life regarding the attitudes, perspectives, and issues you are carrying within your mind and heart, then read His Word to see what He says. Purchase a good study Bible to help you with various questions as you read through Scripture. Find encouragement in the lives of God's men in the Old and New Testaments. Learn what the Father in heaven says about you in the letters of the New

Testament. See the urgency for righteous living in the prophets. Let your heart become opened up to God and learn how to pray as you study the Psalms. Receive God's precious and practical wisdom for life in the Proverbs. Discover the nature of God as you observe Jesus in the gospels. Get into the Word.

If this is brand new for you, I would encourage you to start in the book of Matthew. Read Matthew, Mark, Luke, and John in order. Saturate your mind with the life of Christ. Upon completion of those four books, commonly called *the gospels*, read through the rest of the New Testament. Once finished with that, put a bookmark in Genesis, Matthew again, and the Psalms, and read a little portion of God's Word each day, starting over once you complete it.

Prayer

Watch and pray that you may not enter into temptation. (Matthew 26:41)

The Holy Spirit can help you pray like never before as a new father. I know that when my first daughter was born a renewed sense of urgency entered into my prayer life. I knew the world she was entering into was a broken place filled with hurt and turmoil. I began to pray. As a father, pray hard. Spiritually lead your family by frequently heading to that quiet and private place of prayer. The Bible teaches that all who are covered by the blood of Jesus, all who have placed their faith in His finished work on the cross, can have boldness in approaching God. *"Let us then with confidence draw near to the throne of grace, that we may receive mercy and find grace to help in time of need"* (Hebrews 4:16).

Jesus taught us to pray in His Sermon on the Mount (Matthew 6:9–13). He taught us to:

- Approach God as a loving and perfect Father.
- Worship and honor him.

- Pray for the expansion of his kingdom, including inside your own heart and family.
- Depend on him for your daily provision through prayer.
- Ask him to cleanse you of any and all unrighteousness in your life and heart.
- Petition him to keep you from and through temptation.

However imperfect and incomplete your prayer life might feel, understand that you are praying to a perfect Father in Heaven who is gracious in all His ways. He isn't dependent upon the awesomeness of your prayers but is faithful to work in our lives even when we are weak and faithless. Still, struggle earnestly to grow in your prayer life, making time daily to cry out to your Heavenly Father.

Church

And they devoted themselves to the apostles' teaching and the fellowship, to the breaking of bread and the prayers. (Acts 2:42)

As we noted earlier, both the family and the church are institutions created by God for His own glory and mankind's great benefit. Unfortunately, many families have a less than symbiotic relationship with the church, and vice versa. Some see the church as a place that should/will fix their family, while others see it as a community of far lesser importance than their own family, like a social club or a gym membership. God, however, longs for the church and the family to view each other as mutually and highly beneficial, working together for God's best in both the home and church environments. We should *"not neglect to meet together, as is the habit of some, but encourage one another, and all the more as you see the Day drawing near"* (Hebrews 10:25).

Obviously, new dad, there will be a time and season for rest and recovery for you and more importantly your wife, but this is no time for you to pull away from the body of Christ, the church. Sickness and schedules will make it hard enough for your family to prioritize a church life, but as a father lead your family to your local church community. You likely don't need to take a year off from fellowship and another five years off from church service of any kind. Don't be an MIA guy, removing your family from the church family for the sake of ease. Fight for your family by getting them plugged into your local church community as much as possible. In future years especially, this will be vital. Dear new Dad, allow your family to be refreshed in corporate worship of God, to be instructed in the Word of God, and to be encouraged by the people of God.

Grace

If we are faithless, he remains faithful—for he cannot deny himself. (2 Timothy 2:13)

In all of this it is extremely important for a new father to be encouraged by the grace of God. To be a man, a husband, or a father is to continually run up against your own limitations. I'm sure there are many men out there who could sound like experts in the realm of family life...until they had a family. By the very nature of these callings and relationships you will be tested and stretched beyond your current capabilities. Fortunately, we serve and know a God of wonderful grace and mercy. He lovingly and gently restores us and helps us grow to become the men we long to be. Allow this loving God to have as much access into your life as possible. Avail yourself to Him. By the blood of Jesus, you are His son. He will continually prove His faithfulness to you, helping you become stronger than ever before, the father you've dreamed you could be for your children and family.

Chapter 2

HUSBAND

So Jacob served seven years for Rachel, and they seemed to him but a few days because of the love he had for her. (Genesis 29:20)

Let's rewind the tape and remember how all of this happened in the first place. Somehow, someway, whether in a flash of a moment or through a slow realization over time, you noticed a woman that you wanted to be with. You were struck by her beauty and fascinated by her disposition. You knew she was entirely different from you but so perfectly made for you. Her laughter, her smile, and her silence—all of them stunned you. You came to love her. You knew you wanted to be her husband. You committed yourself to her. You covenanted yourself to her exclusively. She became your wife. You became her husband. You became hers. Either that or you just kind of hooked up. Whatever the case, you are now a husband, and this role is of extreme importance.

Remember, you are a married man. This fact, along with an understanding of the romance required to produce a child in the first place, is often the first thing to be forgotten once a baby enters onto the scene. Couples who were previously lovey-dovey-infatuated with each other can easily kick into survival mode and hunker down for parental duties, forgetting at times that this little baby was a *result* of their love, not a *replacement* for it. I'm not saying this is everyone's experience, nor would I claim this is even a perpetual reality in parenthood, but the early years of a child's life can be very demanding energy-wise. Oftentimes this is compounded by the simple fact that kids often come in bunches, making it not at all uncommon for a family to find themselves with more than a handful of we-can-pretty-much-only-breathe-without-your-help human beings. This can be taxing, especially on a marriage.

None of this is bad. God can use this season in your life in powerful ways. It might be a season where you strip down your priorities to only the most important, which is a good thing to do from time to time. Your motorcycle, golf clubs, and Xbox might have to collect dust for a while. It might be a season where God teaches you radical selflessness, perhaps in a way you've never experienced up to this point. Of course, it will be a season where God uses you to love and nurture a human life, raising her or him up under your care and protection. All of this is good.

This doesn't mean that it comes easy. After the birth of our third daughter, life changed quite extensively. I wouldn't trade those years for anything, but they were definitely physically draining years, years in which we had to roll up our sleeves and do work. In the midst of what can sometimes feel like baby-zone chaos, it is important for a man and a woman to remember that they are husband and wife before they are mom and dad. Forgetting your *marriage* for the sake of your *children* can be lethal.

Your Companion

Then the Lord God said, "It is not good that the man should be alone; I will make him a helper fit for him." (Genesis 2:18)

In the original marriage between Adam and Eve, God declared that it was not good for man to be alone. Even within the Triune Godhead there was friendship, fellowship, and beautiful companionship. Man, however, was initially alone. God cured man's aloneness by creating a woman, a woman who was taken out of his side. Likewise, somewhere along the line the sovereign God solved your aloneness by putting you and your wife together. You are the cure for each other's aloneness. You are to be the best of friends and constant companions. In all of life there is to be no one you are closer to than your bride.

Now, obviously, it isn't going to be as easy to stay up late at night staring into each other's eyes at the local coffee shop as it was when you were engaged, but you have got to fight for that companionship. Husband, when those motherly instincts kick in for your wife, you can be a blessed reminder to her of a previous relationship. You and your wife are going to raise these children and shoot them out of your home like arrows in the hands of the warrior (see Psalms 127:4). They will be gone one day, while you and your bride will live together until death do you part. She might feel tempted to forget marriage and just be a mom, but don't let her do it. Lead her. Love her. Romance her. Help her remember how she even had these kids in the first place.

This isn't to say that your relationship with your wife won't change in some ways with the introduction of children. Time constraints, inconsistent sleeping patterns, and dirty diapers all have a way of constraining a free-flowing companionship. That said, this can be a wonderfully deepening time in your relationship together. Handled well, this season could grow your love for one another, strengthen your communication toward each other, and improve your ability to serve the other's needs. But get your game face on and take the gentle and loving lead by continuing to cultivate and develop your companionship with your bride.

Your Priority

Therefore a man shall leave his father and his mother and hold fast to his wife, and they shall become one flesh. (Genesis 2:24)

After creating the woman as a companion for the man, God officiated the first wedding. At that original ceremony, God made a declaration regarding every future marriage. He stated that a man would leave his family and begin to hold fast to his wife, becoming one flesh with her. Though they were previously two distinct individuals and obviously could still function in individualistic ways even after marriage, God declared they would become one.

Now, you might be close with your college friends or your fishing buddies, and you might really enjoy your Monday night football crew, but you will never have this kind of relationship with them. You will never be one with any other person outside of your bride. Your identities are now so closely tied to one another that God sees you as one flesh. The sexual act has consummated your relationship, putting you together, and has now brought forth a child. And you will never be one with any friend or family member, including your very own children, like you are one with your wife.

I find that danger creeps into a marriage when the oneness of their relationship begins to be tested. When the husband and wife begin to act like individuals once again, living separate lives from one another, unwilling to open up their hearts to one another, the devil can more easily find a foothold for attack (see Ephesians 4:27 NIV). Additionally, there is also the danger of trying to have oneness with a broad circle of family and friends, relegating your marriage to a distant second place in order of priority and importance. All this is common during the child-raising and childbearing years. As a husband, be sure to set your marriage as the priority, holding fast to your wife as the Scripture says. Don't allow any other family member higher priority than your wife, and especially make sure you aren't cultivating oneness with any other woman, such as a co-worker or church friend. Your wife is yours. You are hers. You are one. Act like it.

This will look differently at different seasons of your marriage, especially during the years you are raising children and beginning right there during the labor and delivery. Your wife's best friend and mother didn't impregnate her, so be sure to talk through how your hospital visit is going to go, making certain to protect a little time for just you and her. Over the first few weeks there might be visitors, many of whom will be greatly welcomed by you as they will be of assistance, but make sure you and your bride have opportunities to be alone with your baby and with each other. At times you might need to run interference and protect her blind side, telling various friends and family members that you guys just need some space.

Over the next few months and even years, the challenge to your oneness likely won't be as much from without as from within. The challenge of raising babies can easily drive the friendship, companionship, and romance out of a marriage. Be sure to date her, pursue her, love her, vacation with her, and open your heart to her. Treat her like a woman, the love of your life, not just a mother.

Your Perspective

Likewise, husbands, live with your wives in an understanding way, showing honor to the woman as the weaker vessel, since they are heirs with you of the grace of life, so that your prayers may not be hindered. (1 Peter 3:7)

I realize I'll probably get myself into trouble with some people for quoting the verse above (1 Peter 3:7). In trouble with wives, because it refers to them as the weaker vessel. In trouble with husbands, because it tells them to understand their wives! I write in jest, of course, as every Word from the Holy Spirit found in Scripture is true and good.

Husbands are told to *live with their wives in an understanding way. Honor* is to flow from husbands toward their wives. There ought to be a comprehension that they are *coheirs of the grace of life.* During the earliest years of a marriage, especially once children come onto the scene, this *understanding* and *honor* are absolutely vital. You have an opportunity to honor your wife and dwell with her with understanding. Your gentle care and concern is of extreme importance during the early years of raising a family.

Christina, my wife, is a naturally gifted mother. She has an emotional strength and inner resolve that enables her to adeptly mother our children. To me, she is a born natural. She works so diligently and tirelessly to mother our daughters. On top of all of that, my wife is a godly woman. She truly loves Jesus, as is evidenced by her love for His Word, her love for prayer, and her love for His church. Still, Christina has always needed me to remind her of who she truly is. It is so easy for a woman to identify herself so closely with her children, sometimes to an unhealthy extreme. A good husband is able to lovingly remind his bride through his words, his actions, and his priorities toward her that she is first a daughter of God, as well as a woman and a wife.

In some ways, at certain times, your wife may need you to rescue her from an unhealthy perspective about herself. This isn't to be done with blunt-force trauma, but prayerfully and gently. Mothering is a tender role in many ways, and the world we are raising our children in is full of danger, which can lead a mother to serious fright, so don't recklessly or carelessly insult your bride if she has slipped into a wrong perspective. A spirit-filled husband will patiently honor his wife, reminding her of her identity in Christ and her womanhood, all the while understanding where she is coming from. He will tenderly love her and treat her with respect, enabling her to take a breath from time to time and realize that she is this man's wife.

Your Patience

Husbands, love your wives, and do not be harsh with them. (Colossians 3:19)

The stress of child raising leads some husbands, however, to behave completely contrary to Scripture. They become irritated with their wives, jealous of the attention given to their children, and frustrated that the relationship has devolved into a workmanlike struggle to feed, clothe, and bathe this newfound miracle of a life. This is often a symptom of a man who was merely looking for a replacement for his own mother, someone to nurture and clothe and feed him, instead of a wife. Rather than act *proactively* like a leader would, he reacts to the situation like a child would and grows angry with his bride. He lashes out or broods within, upset that the romance and relationship are not as they used to be.

Paul tells us not to be harsh with our wives, instead loving them. Your bride does not need your anger or your impatience; she needs your love.

There will be a natural learning curve as children begin to grow up inside your home. There will be moments and seasons of imbalance, moments where the marriage is seemingly set aside for the sake of the child. There will be moments and seasons when romance seems to be at a low ebb as a result of your offspring. Your job is not to harshly rage against this potential reality, but to lovingly husband and lead your bride back into companionship and oneness.

Be patient with your wife. She will need to demonstrate extreme patience toward you in your new role as a father, so extend the grace and honor of an understanding heart toward her. Even though it might seem as if she has come preprogrammed with every skill and piece of information necessary to parent your children, the reality is that she is learning on the fly just like everyone else. Lovingly guide her and lead her. Just as your Father in heaven has extended and will extend such amazing grace toward you, extend that same grace toward your wife. If you lead without a harsh and critical spirit, the two of you will figure it out and get back onto the same page.

Chapter 3

SERVANT

And he sat down and called the twelve. And he said to them, "If anyone would be first, he must be last of all and servant of all." (Mark 9:35)

Jesus *taught* servant-leadership with His Words and *exemplified* servant-leadership through His life. He told His disciples that the first must be the last, the greatest must be the least, and the master must be the servant. The night He was arrested and tried, on the eve of the most brutal death imaginable, Jesus washed the feet of His disciples, an illustration of extreme service. In that moment He said, *"For I have given you an example, that you also should do just as I have done to you"* (John 13:15). Jesus's selfless act of service should stand, for every man of God, every husband who names the name of Christ, and every father who seeks to raise his children for the Lord, as the ultimate illustration of selfless service and sacrificial love.

When Paul wrote to the Philippian church he exhorted them to *"do nothing from selfish ambition or conceit, but in humility count others more significant than yourselves. Let each of you look not only to his own interests, but also to the interests of others"* (Philippians 2:3–4). He knew their joy would be full and strong and rich if only they would live outside of themselves. He longed for them to serve one another. In searching for a fitting illustration to hammer home his point, Paul dropped one of the greatest statements in all of God's Word regarding the incarnation of Christ. He told them to *"Have this mind among yourselves, which is yours in Christ Jesus, who, though he was in the form of God, did not count equality with God a thing to be grasped, but emptied himself, by taking the form of a servant, being born in the likeness of men. And being found in human form, he humbled himself by becoming obedient to the point of death, even death on a cross"* (Philippians 2:5–8).

Husband, notice the extreme humiliation of Christ for His bride. Notice the ways in which He lowered Himself for us. Firstly, *"He did not count equality with God a thing to be grasped"* (v. 6). Jesus, the second person of the Triune Godhead, God Himself, did not count His rights and position as something to hold onto, something to grasp for. He let go. He was still God, but He allowed Himself to become humbled for us. All too often a husband and father will lock in on his rights, position, and privileges. Any slight or sign of disrespect sets him off. His insecurity is glaring. The godly father, however, is willing to let go of his rights in order to sacrificially serve his family.

Secondly, Jesus *"emptied Himself"* (v. 7), a statement pregnant with profound theological implications. Observe other Bible translations for a moment, just to allow this truth to sink into your heart and mind. Jesus *"made Himself nothing"* (NIV), *"made Himself of no reputation"* (NKJV), and *"gave up His divine privileges"* (NLT). Obviously, Jesus retained His deity, for that could not be shaken from Him, but this Royal King of all Kings divested Himself of His glory and became a man for us. If Jesus could step out of heaven and into our mess in order to die for us, I'm sure more of us fathers could put down the remote, get off the couch, and change a diaper.

Notice thirdly how Jesus emptied Himself *"by taking the form of a servant"* (v. 7). Jesus humbled Himself to serve the Father's will, but also to serve the great need of a lost and broken mankind. Remember, Paul is holding Jesus out as our example, an inspirational reminder that we should not look only to our *"own interests, but also to the interests of others"* (v. 4). We are to serve. As fathers, it is important to see ourselves as servants within the home. Raising children is an extremely servant-oriented task. It will take years of work. I will never forget a friend of mine telling me that since the Jewish day began at sundown the night before, he tried to come home at the end of his work day feeling fresh, like it was a brand-new day to serve his family. At the end of a long day, you might want to come home and relax, but that just might be the time you are most needed. You might need to roll up your sleeves and play with, listen to, feed, nurture, speak with, read to, clean, or watch your kids. You might be needed in the morning or called upon in the middle of the night. Babies and children don't have on/off switches, so get ready to be a servant.

Observe fourthly how Jesus was *"born in the likeness of men"* (v. 7). God became a man. For us. The God who formed and created everything became flesh and dwelt among us (see Colossians 1:16, John 1:14). When my daughters look to the sky at night and are overtaken by the beauty of the stars, I remember that the God who made those stars became a man for me. What a servant! What love! Jesus stooped down for us. What great distance He traveled to serve and save us. Let me ask you, father: in order to serve your wife and children, would you have to travel a greater distance than Christ? Of course not. If Jesus traveled that great a distance, any distance we would go to lower ourselves and serve another is far less a journey.

Fifthly, notice how *"being found in human form, He humbled Himself by becoming obedient"* (v. 8). That Jesus incarnated was humiliation enough, but He was born into a deeply humble situation. Born in a barn, raised in relative poverty, and toiling for years in obedient anonymity, Jesus did not live the life of royalty. He was abased in all ways. Not only was He a man, He was a humble man. He truly lowered Himself for those He loved.

And sixthly, consider how far His obedience ran: *"to the point of death"* (v. 8). Jesus was willing to die for those He loved. What great love! Who could ever love like Christ? Here we come face to face with our great need for the Holy Spirit to live within and empower us as fathers. *"If the Spirit of him who raised Jesus from the dead dwells in you, he who raised Christ Jesus from the dead will also give life to your mortal bodies through his Spirit who dwells in you"* (Romans 8:11). You might not ever have an opportunity to actually *die* for your family, but you will have many opportunities, daily, to die to yourself for your family.

Lastly, observe the type of death Jesus submitted Himself to: *"even death on a cross"* (v. 8). His wasn't a death of old age, sickness, or some more merciful form of capital punishment. No, Jesus endured the most shameful and horrible kind of death imaginable when He endured the cross. Now He says to all, *"If anyone would come after me, let him deny himself and take up his cross daily and follow me"* (Luke 9:23). As dads, we are called daily to lay down our lives for our families. We are to spiritually, emotionally, and physically give ourselves up for our families. We belong to them. Finances, hobbies, and schedules should all be seen through this lens. This is the bottom line. We are to serve our families like Christ served us.

Your Service

There are times, however, when our service kicks into high gear. There are ebbs and flows, ups and downs, seasons in this life. I'm sure marriage has helped you develop a stronger selflessness, a deeper regard for others, and an understanding that you are called to lay down your life, but children will take it to a whole new level. In marriage you might have found that your bank account went from "mine" to "ours" overnight, but with kiddos you'll find it shift into the "theirs" column. In all seriousness, children are an incredible blessing from God, and one reason for this is that they really help us live an others-centered life, something that ultimately brings us incredible joy.

I absolutely love being a father. The thrill of watching my children grow and mature right before my eyes never gets old to me. They fascinate me. I could watch them for hours. They bring me such delight. For everything I put into them, I receive so much more. The laughter never stops. The love always flows. They are the joy of my life.

Still, bringing up children takes great service, and the earliest years are no exception. There will be loss of sleep. Free time may dissipate. Hobbies might quickly become impractical. Friendships may have to shift. There will be times God wants you to simply rescue your wife. Man the ship. Let her rest.

I would encourage you to prepare your mind and heart to serve in *physical ways*. You will be called upon to wake up in the night, run errands, and change diapers. Whatever your household duties are before children, expect to step up your game because you will be needed more around the home. Christina, who was an elementary school teacher before our first daughter was born, and I have been blessed with the opportunity for her to stay home to raise our children throughout the week. This meant that we talked through and planned out our nighttime routine with each child. Since I would be required to head to an office each morning, she routinely would wake to feed the children during the night, but this didn't mean I was off the hook completely. There were plenty of nights I would help out, not to mention the early mornings when I could wake up early and allow her to sleep in as long as possible. There were seasons we felt like zombies. Be prepared to take on responsibilities that are new to you. Serve.

I would also encourage you to prepare you mind and heart to serve in *emotional ways* as well. Having babies, raising children, and being a mother can be a psychologically draining experience, and your ability to serve your wife in the emotional realm is of the utmost importance. At times you will be called upon to just open up your heart and talk with her about your life, work, and perspectives. She might simply need your companionship. At other times you might need to arrange to free up her time and schedule to be able to visit with some of her friends or family, even if just for an hour or two. Often you will be required to simply listen. When the time to listen to your bride presents itself, be all in. Don't have one eye on the game and another on your iPhone, giving your wife only partial attention. Be fully there.

I would also encourage you to prepare your mind and heart to serve in *spiritual ways* as well. Your family needs you as the spiritual leader. In reality, you are the spiritual leader, for better or for worse, whether you like it or not. If you are spiritually dead, you will lead your family in that direction, but if you are spiritually alive, you will lead them toward spiritual life. It just happens. Be the spiritual servant in the home. This doesn't mean that you have to have a daily 4:00 a.m. prayer meeting with your wife or begin teaching the Pentateuch to your two-month-old, but you are called to care for and serve your family spiritually. Tell your wife about what you've been reading in your Bible, pray for your entire family, and lead them to be a part of your local church family. I am so proud of the many great men and women in my home church who have not allowed the birth of a child to keep them from corporate worship for very long. Amazing.

A Rewarding Experience

At the beginning of this chapter we studied a portion of Philippians 2, observing the extreme humility of Christ as He incarnated and laid down His life for us. What we didn't study there was the result of Jesus's humiliation, His death upon the cross. Paul wrote, *"Therefore God has highly exalted him and bestowed on him the name that is above every name, so that at the name of Jesus every knee should bow, in heaven and on earth and under the earth, and every tongue confess that Jesus Christ is Lord, to the glory of God the Father"* (Philippians 2:9–11). In short, Jesus has been highly exalted by the Father as a result of stepping out of eternity into our mess in order to serve us so well.

That said, it is also true that serving your wife and children well is an incredibly rewarding experience. They will be glad and you will have joy. Self will fade and Jesus will increase in you (see John 3:30). As you humble yourself, God will exalt you, quite often in the eyes of the very people you are serving (see James 4:10). You and I will never serve perfectly like Christ did, but through the help of His Spirit we become more able than ever before. Lean into Him. Trust Him. Ask for His grace to enable you as you seek to serve.

Chapter 4

LEADER

But I want you to understand that the head of every man is Christ, the head of a wife is her husband, and the head of Christ is God. (1 Corinthians 11:3)

Recently Christina and I were having a little family church session with our girls when an interesting conversation ensued with the three of them. We had been reading in the gospel of Mark regarding the selection of Jesus's twelve disciples. It was so much fun listening to my seven-year-old as she tried to pronounce some of the names on that list. After talking about a few other observations, Christina asked the girls, "Do you think it's fair that all of Jesus's apostles were men and not women?" Leave it to my wife to ask an amazing question like that! The girls all sat there thinking about it. They slowly confessed that they thought it was fair, mostly because they know Jesus to be good and just, especially as is evidenced on the cross, so surely He wouldn't behave in an unfair manner.

I then asked them if they thought men were better than women or if boys were better than girls. That question didn't take them long to answer as they all shouted at me, in the strongest possible terms, that men and boys were in no way superior to women and girls. On the contrary, they argued, they are equal. I then asked them if God the Father and God the Son are equal. They affirmed the equality within the Triune Godhead. Then I asked them if Jesus, God the Son, had been obedient to the Father. Had the Father led the Son? They affirmed that, yes, He had. I asked them if that made Jesus of lesser quality than the Father. They correctly asserted that He is equal to the Father and the Spirit.

In other words, even though men and women are created equal in the sight of God, just as there are roles within the Godhead, so are there different roles between husbands and wives in a marriage. A husband is never greater in quality, but he is called to be the leader. Paul stated as much to the Corinthians: *"But I want you to understand that the head of every man is Christ, the head of a wife is her husband, and the head of Christ is God"* (1 Corinthians 11:3). The proper order is clear. Jesus leads you; you submit and surrender to Him; you give Him full access and rule in your life. Then, you are to lovingly and gently lead your bride.

It is extremely unfortunate that many men, however, are bullies to their wives. They never serve. They never listen. They never tenderly care for their wives. Instead they abusively pummel their wives, sometimes even misappropriating Scriptures about her submission and his leadership! These self-willed cowards forget that their leadership is to mirror the leadership of Christ. They are to be sacrificial, loving, giving themselves up in death for their brides. *"Husbands, love your wives, as Christ loved the church and gave himself up for her"* (Ephesians 5:25). Give yourself up for your bride, husband. Lay yourself down for your family, father.

That said, it is still important for a dad to understand his role of leadership within the home. We are called to serve, but we are to be servant-leaders. Unfortunately, especially in the area of parenthood, men are often portrayed and seen as unknowledgeable at best and moronic at worst, but you are to be involved as a leader inside of your home.

Manager

The apostle Paul wrote many of the epistles of the New Testament. Three of these letters were dedicated to two pastors named Timothy and Titus. As pastors, these men were required to lead and oversee the body of Christ. In Paul's first letter to Timothy, he outlined the prerequisites for those who would be involved in spiritual leadership within the church in the future. He first detailed the characteristics of pastors, spiritual men overseeing the spiritual matters of the church, and then detailed the characteristics of deacons, spiritual men overseeing the physical matters of the church.

Concerning pastors, Paul wrote, *"He must manage his own household well, with all dignity keeping his children submissive, for if someone does not know how to manage his own household, how will he care for God's church?"* (1 Timothy 3:4–5). This isn't the only requirement Paul listed, but it is fascinating to see the Holy Spirit's concern for the pastor and his family. Additionally, Paul spoke of the deacons in this way: *"Let deacons each be the husband of one wife, managing their children and their own households well"* (1 Timothy 3:12). In other words, the deacons were called to have an upstanding family life along with the pastors.

Notice the word Paul used for both of these offices: *manage.* These spiritual men, men who were to live lives worth imitation, were called to superintend, preside over, protect, care for, give attention to, and lead their families—to manage their households and children. This style of leadership in the home isn't to be found exclusively among pastors and deacons, but is to be the aim of every Christian home and man. To *manage* the family is the perfect word to describe this fatherly role. To manage well a father and husband does not need to be involved in the smallest of details, but should be involved in the larger-scale decisions that are made within the home, even in moments when he is deferring to the expertise or counsel of another, particularly his own bride.

Unfortunately, many men feel as if they have no permission to "manage their children" or their "own households" at all (1 Timothy 3:12). By listening to the ridiculing voice of culture and the doubts of insecurity in their own minds, many men believe they have nothing to offer when it comes to leadership among their children or home. Many a father will automatically defer to his wife, forcing her to occupy a role she was not designed for. A mother is called to love her husband and her children, but to be placed in the sole leadership position of the family is unbiblical and unhealthy for her.

Don't get me wrong. Your wife is going to have an incredible amount of wisdom when it comes to leading the children and creating the household you both desire. She will likely think and pray long and hard about each decision made regarding your children, often foreseeing the distant outcomes of today's decisions generations before they come to pass. There will be thousands of times a simple "yes, dear" will be enough. Your wife will likely think through various parenting styles and perspectives. Her motherly wisdom will likely be beyond compare. Still, you are called to lead, especially in the major and significant philosophical decisions regarding your family. You must be involved. You must *manage.*

Key Decisions

There are a million decisions to make when it comes to bringing up a family. As a husband and father, you are to lovingly lead discussion with your wife, receive counsel and wisdom from others, and study God's Word in order to come to the conclusions that are right for you and your family. Unfortunately, many have presented an exclusive "right way" for various aspects of the home and family, instead of recognizing and honoring the variety in cultures, temperaments, and backgrounds that lead to a diversity of wise decisions regarding a home. Scripture stresses the need for love, honor, and discipline within the home, but individual couples will have freedom when it comes to applying these principles in their context. That said, Scripture does not give the father permission to abdicate his leadership role within the home.

You will be involved in key decisions for your family. Seek the Lord in prayer, His Word, and in counsel from older and wiser believers whom you respect. Become willing to admit you don't know or have the answers. Receive the wisdom God gives to your bride. Humble yourself. If you do, your leadership and decision making will be excellent and such a blessing to your wife and children. Here are a few key areas in which you will likely find yourself making decisions:

Family Structure. Hopefully, these are matters you have already discussed, but there is a structural philosophy to your family that you and your bride must agree upon. While our culture sometimes frowns upon a woman devoting herself primarily to work inside the home rather than outside of it, Scripture exhorts a young woman to love her husband and children and to work at home (see Titus 2:4–5). Paul has strong words for those who would refuse to care for their families, stating bluntly, *"But if anyone does not provide for his relatives, and especially for members of his household, he has denied the faith and is worse than an unbeliever"* (1 Timothy 5:8). In a less agrarian and often urban or suburban world, it is important for a husband and wife to come together, set priorities, and decide what their family structure will look like when it comes to employment and provision. The weight of this burden should fall most squarely, if not entirely, upon the husband.

Child Development. There are numerous philosophies readily available to the modern parent. Equipped with a trusty Internet connection, you will be able to find 1,001 often conflicting ideas on how to develop a newborn into a fully functioning adult. Many of these decisions are thrust upon us at the outset and can be quite overwhelming. Do I put my baby on a more rigid feeding schedule, or should I feed her whenever she seems to be hungry? Is he to sleep in our bed with us or in his own bassinet or crib and eventually in his own room? Are we going to supplement her diet with formula? Will it be organic? Is he allergic to gluten? It can all be a little much. To be candid, I am more of a sleep-with-my-wife-without-my-kids-putting-a-damper-on-the-experience kind of guy, but if you decide to co-sleep with your kids, you had better be involved in the decision. Don't tune me out for telling you what we've done in our home. I'm only asking you to lovingly lead your family. Come to agreement with your bride, if possible. Be involved with and in the decision-making process.

Disciplinary Method. *Method* is probably the worst word to use here. We love to find methods, trust methods, and worship methods, but God sent His Son who gave us His Spirit so we wouldn't have to always trust a bunch of methods. Instead, we are able to grow in the megacharacteristics He desires for us, things like love, consistency, faithfulness, and the ability to nurture. Still, it is good for parents to decide on a style of discipline together. Just remember that Jesus is the one who has to save your kids, not a workbook you bought on Amazon. Remember your Father in heaven. His discipline is **consistent**, so create a predictable style of discipline versus an arbitrary style where children have no idea what will and will not be punished. Don't use empty words, promising discipline but never delivering it. Additionally, create a style of discipline that is **age-appropriate** for your children. You can't make your two-year-old stay home from prom, nor should you tell your teenager to fold his hands for a silent time-out. Also, allow yourself to be **child-flexible** when it comes to your discipline style. We all want a method that works for every child, but your kids will come out of the womb freakishly different from one another, so remember the goal of discipline, the future you are trying to lead them to, and be flexible. Discipline should always be forward looking and future oriented. Additionally, remember that your discipline must stem from love and relationship, not anger and position, so cultivate your own heart and tender relationship with your children.

Communication

Parenting is hard work. It doesn't just happen. You will need to spend time and energy in researching and preparing yourself for the various stages of your child's life. You will need to spend hours in conversation with your bride. You will need to discuss each individual child and his or her tendencies. You will need to be involved in creating a household and structure that is conducive to your child's development and progress.

In all of this, it will become highly important for you to communicate regularly with your bride. Open your heart and tell her what you see. Open your ears and listen to her thoughts and perspectives. Open your eyes and watch the progress of your children. If you can continue to communicate with your wife over these matters, you need not become overwhelmed with the enormity of the task. Instead, adjust, grow, and adapt yourself to the current environment you find yourself in. Parenting is quite often a game of tweaking, and you are involved in this leadership process.

One of my favorite professional sports to watch on television—and by watch on television I mean fall asleep on the couch to—is Major League

Baseball. I love learning and watching the strategy involved in this incredibly complex game. While it is the players who determine the outcome of the games, quite often the managers must make crucial decisions that heavily influence the results. These managers are thinking men. They are constantly observing, watching, and studying. They receive counsel from the bench coaches and various specialists. They statistically analyze each and every situation. And they make decisions. They lead.

What a wonderful opportunity we have to manage and lead our households well! We have an opportunity to be such a joy and a blessing to our families. Our gentle leadership and loving care can be so helpful to every individual inside of our home. Father, remember that you are a leader. Lead well.

Chapter 5

DAD

The righteous who walks in his integrity—blessed are his children after him!
(Proverbs 20:7)

Every person on the face of the earth is shaped by his or her father. For good or for bad, for better or worse, dads influence their children. There is a seeming importance in everything a father does and says toward their children. We grow up watching our dads, what they do and don't do, what they say and what they don't say. We want to know what makes them tick. We want to understand their value system. We want to hear their approval. We watch them like a hawk.

Statistics and cultural analysis will not allow us to downplay the role of the father. We know of his importance. It is staring us in the face. The gravity of the father's role can lead us to panic or passion. We can either become terrified or emboldened. Fear would cause us to dismiss the significance of a strong and healthy father. Our own insecurity, perhaps brought on by secret sin, might cause us to act as if being a dad really isn't as important as people make it out to be. We ought not to dismiss this responsibility and task too easily. Instead, we should grow excited at the possibilities in front of us. To be a father is to have great influence and power, something that a man can easily use for good in the life of his child.

Perhaps you are a man whose wife is expecting your first child in a matter of months. Maybe a handful of little ones are already populating your residence. As you meditate upon the radical sway fathers are reported to have among their children, perhaps fear wells up inside you. You might even be thinking of the impact of your own father on your life, negatively or positively, and are terrified at that level of responsibility. Note, however, that God is for you and has modeled for you the influence of a perfect

Father. Not only that, but He is gracious and good toward you and has brought you this far. Declare His praises, rejoice at where you stand today, and move forward. Receive His grace, believe and trust Him for great things in the lives of your children, and rest assured that He has the power and might to strengthen you for the task at hand.

On the other hand, this great influence could be considered a wonderful gift from the hand of God. A multitude of voices will shout at our children throughout their entire lives, so it is nice to know that the voice of the father is so strong and loud and powerful. In a world that will plead for your children's devotion, it is good to realize the influence you can have upon your kids. The key, however, is to use that influence and voice for their edification from the very beginning. When we do, we embed something powerful into our children and, generally speaking, fortify them for the future as the Proverbs state: *"Train up a child in the way he should go; even when he is old he will not depart from it"* (Proverbs 22:6). This starts from the very beginning.

Know God

I am writing to you, fathers, because you know him who is from the beginning...
(1 John 2:13–14)

The relative silence of God's Word concerning the role of parents has always been interesting to me. This isn't to say that God hasn't left us scriptural witness concerning what it means to be a mother and a father, but only that I would initially expect much more of God's written Word to be devoted to teaching on the family. Like maybe after the gospels (Matthew through John) we could get the books of First and Second Parentonians or something. As is often the case in Holy Scripture, however, God has an ability all His own to say the most pointed and foundational things in the most succinct of terms. What man often tries to say regarding parenting through countless conferences, books, support groups, and podcasts, usually with the sincerest of hearts, God is able to say perfectly with a few short strokes. He is able to get at the very core of the issue.

Additionally, I think God knows something we often overlook. God devotes the pages of Scripture to the story of redemption and restoration, how He has made a way for mankind to enter back into relationship and fellowship with Him. He gives us the gospel and speaks to us of our new identity in Christ. In our haste to become better parents we often rush to self-help models and topical sermon series, passing over the simple fact that God is looking to make us whole again. He wants to restore us, to sanctify us, to transform us from the inside out (see Hebrews 8:10). When this relationship with God is ongoing and real, our children are exceedingly blessed. I'm not advocating a superspiritual pie-in-the-sky approach to parenting, but we simply must not skip over the fact that God is looking to make us into healthy people through and through. This internal health can and will benefit our children. To be armed with a few parenting principles, yet lack a relationship with God that is growing and vital, is dangerous and will lead to our children's discouragement.

So I encourage you once again, father, to prioritize your relationship with the God and Father of heaven. Abide in Christ (see John 15). Learn to hear from Him in the pages of His Word. Learn to cry out to Him in the prayers of your heart. Learn to be corrected and tweaked by your Heavenly Father.

Encourage

Fathers, do not provoke your children, lest they become discouraged.
(Colossians 3:21)

All that said, the Bible has quite a bit to say concerning fatherhood. The Bible is filled with wonderful examples of solid fathers like Noah, Abraham, and Phillip. It is also filled with pictures of fathers who struggled at times, men like Eli, Job, and even David. There is much learning to be found regarding fatherhood in the pages of the historical records in the Old Testament and the law of the Old Covenant. Wisdom regarding fatherhood can be found in the pages of the poetic literature. Yes, the Bible does speak to dads.

Some of the strongest words for fathers, however, especially new fathers, are found in two simple exhortations from Paul the apostle to the Colossian and the Ephesian churches. His directive to the fathers in Colossae is noted above, and his Ephesian version is strikingly similar: *"Fathers, do not provoke your children to anger, but bring them up in the discipline and instruction of the Lord"* (Ephesians 6:4).

In both passages Paul tells believing fathers they have the potential to provoke their children. When a father breaks a promise, offers a word of insult, or is generally unsupportive, it can lead to the provocation of his children. Kids will be stirred up, lash out, and have general unrest. Perhaps you've seen a little child, or a grown man for that matter, lash out at someone or something and have determined that something deeper must have affected his heart. Oftentimes this is the result of being provoked by his very own father. This never excuses anyone's personal sin, but I believe many crimes against God and man have occurred in response to the provocation of a father.

One of the easiest ways for a Christian father to provoke his children is through hypocrisy. Naming the name of Christ yet living like the devil is no way to garner respect and admiration from your kids. Fortunately, when your children are brand spanking new, they will have a hard time distinguishing the dichotomy in your life. Consider this a grace period, a season where you can get on track in your obedience to Christ before they realize what's really going on.

Further, Paul concludes that *provoked* children will become *discouraged* children, so it seems reasonable that fathers are called to encourage their children with their lives and actions. If hypocrisy, a harsh tone, and an inconsistent lifestyle will become discouraging to your children, then the opposite will bring them great encouragement and health. Walk before them with sincerity. Even at an early age, apologize to them when necessary. Speak to them softly, building them up with your words. When you speak of the importance of Jesus Christ, show them the importance of Jesus Christ with your lifestyle. Over time, your children will grow more and more encouraged through your soft and loving leadership over their lives. The last thing our children need is a rigid Pharisee of a father. No, they need a grace-filled and Spirit-filled man who will lovingly lead them like Jesus Christ would lead them.

Words: The Apostle Paul

For you know how, like a father with his children, we exhorted each one of you and encouraged you and charged you to walk in a manner worthy of God, who calls you into his own kingdom and glory. (1 Thessalonians 2:11–12)

Although, at first glance, the Bible does not seem to be replete with admonitions, directions, and specifics about fatherhood, God's Word and the ministry of God's men continually take an overtly fatherly tone. In fact, as noted in the Scripture above, the apostles themselves often did ministry to cities and local churches as fathers. So, in one sense, as we watch their leadership in the early church, we can observe how to lead our own homes and families.

Notice immediately how Paul tells the Thessalonian church that he ministered to them *"like a father with his children"* (2:11). Had this been his only explanation of his fatherly role toward them, we might be left to guess at how this unfolded in Thessalonica. Paul, however, continued to explain to them that he had exhorted, encouraged, and charged each one of them. What should leap off the page at this point is the reality that *Paul used his words* to conduct his fatherly role with the Thessalonian believers. In other words, in the mind of this brilliant apostle, a man who was certainly very in tune with the thoughts and will of God, a father was a man who used his words to build up his children, developing them into the people God desired them to be.

New Dad, please understand the power of your words at the very outset. From the very beginning of your child's life, you need to speak to them. Your words must encourage them, direct them, and upbuild them. Your words have great power. Your words will shape your children. Open up your heart and your mouth and speak to your kids.

Let's look more closely at the specific words Paul used to describe his fatherly chats with the Thessalonian church. Firstly, he told them that he had *exhorted* them, a word that speaks of calling up to one's side in order to urge someone on. A good father will call his children closely to himself and speak to them. These aren't brutal commands from a distance, but exhortations that flow from relationship and fellowship. From the very beginning, your child should grow to know of your lap as a place of safety, love, and encouragement. Set the tone and allow them to grow up in a home where they expect to have time sitting in your presence, enjoying interactions with you, and being built up as you speak into their lives. Obviously, in the beginning years they might not understand your words, but they will understand your warmth, tone, and interest in them. Your investment in this time at the earliest of ages will pay huge dividends later on down the line.

Secondly, Paul told the Thessalonian church that he had *encouraged* them. This is a word that indicates consolation, comfort, and the ability to cheer up an individual. The idea is that of taking a discouraged heart and refilling it with good cheer and great courage. This means, obviously, that Mom will not be the only source of encouragement in the family, a sort of good cop, bad cop experience. No, while a father's words will have a masculine tone and a male perspective, they are to be, overall, incredibly encouraging. I'm sure it is possible to see some immediate results by being harsh and condescending toward your children, but over the long haul you will see the greatest fruit come from being an encouraging man.

The final word Paul used to describe his fatherly ministry to the Thessalonian church was the word *charged*. This is a fascinating word because it literally means to testify. Think of this in a courtroom setting. What are the two things someone offering testimony does in that environment? For one, she simply retells her own experiences. Your children need to hear you throughout their entire lives speak of the lessons you are learning, the ways God is speaking to you, and the great things He has done throughout your entire life. Secondly, someone offering testimony is merely answering questions in a courtroom scene. A good father will allow his children the freedom and space to ask a multitude of questions. This takes time, energy, and will, but it is greatly worth it.

Words: The Apostle John

The apostle John's entire ministry was fatherly. A man far different from the apostle Paul, John seemed to continually brim over with love. His short letter of First John was written entirely from a fatherly perspective. In fact, one great study of the role of a dad is to look at the different times John used the phrase *little children* in his first epistle. Notice the progression:

"My little children, I am writing these things to you so that you may not sin. But if anyone does sin, we have an advocate with the Father, Jesus Christ the righteous" (1 John 2:1). As a father speaking to his own little children, there were two main things John wanted his readers to know. Firstly, he longed to speak to them of a life that was free from sin. He was willing to warn them, instruct them, and talk to them freely of the dangers around them. You have an opportunity as a dad to teach your children of the gravity of sin throughout their young lives. As you do, always remember that your goal isn't merely to have behavior changed for the now, but to foster a person prepared for the future. I can still remember my first conversation, heavily filtered and guarded, with my firstborn daughter about the local porn shop. I kept it very age appropriate, but as we drove by I wanted her to know of the dangers there and the prayers of her father for that place to close down. Secondly, John wanted them to know of the grace of God. When they sinned, John wanted them to know of the great advocate they had with the

Father in heaven, Jesus Christ the righteous. Continually give your children grace. Show them grace. Discipline them well, but give them the hope of the glorious gospel of Jesus Christ. When they confront face to face the weakness within them and their own propensity to sin—something they might begin to see around seven or eight years of age—talk to them of the wonderful internal work of Jesus Christ. He can transform them!

John also wrote, *"I am writing to you, little children, because your sins are forgiven for his name's sake"* (1 John 2:12). John spoke to them of the greatness of God's name, namely that God's reputation is wonderful because of the forgiveness of sins offered through the cross of Christ. Always bring your children back to the cross. Let them filter their questions about the universe and world and Word of God through the cross of Jesus Christ. Do everything you can to make sure that God's name is honored within your home (Matthew 6:9). Let Jesus be famous within the walls of your house.

"And now, little children, abide in him..." (1 John 2:28). Here John progresses into talking to his little children about their personal relationship with Jesus, and he harkens back to the Words of Christ: *"Abide in me, and I in you. As the branch cannot bear fruit by itself, unless it abides in the vine, neither can you, unless you abide in me"* (John 15:4). I know I've plucked this one string quite a bit in this little book, fathers, but Jesus wants a relationship with you. He longs for you to remain in constant life-receiving relationship with Him for the purpose of bearing more fruit and much fruit, which glorifies the Father and blesses others. At different levels and stages of your children's lives, like John, speak to them about abiding in Christ. Demonstrate it for them. Be infatuated with and connected to Christ and they will never forget it.

"Little children, let no one deceive you. Whoever practices righteousness is righteous, as he is righteous" (1 John 3:7). Additionally, John spoke of a lifestyle of righteous living. As a father, you have an opportunity to embed a value system inside of your children. How will they feel about the poor and the abandoned? What will their view of church service be? How will

they define personal consecration? Many of these definitions will come from their father.

"Little children, let us not love in word or talk but in deed and in truth" (1 John 3:18). John stressed the preeminence of love in his ministry to his spiritual children. Cultivate a culture of love and honor within your home. Teach them how they are to love God, family, and the body of Christ through your words, but also with your actions.

"Little children, you are from God and have overcome them, for he who is in you is greater than he who is in the world" (1 John 4:4). Again, John references the reality of the battle at hand. Especially as your children grow older, they will come face to face with the pressures and influences around them. To ignore this would be folly. Instead, like John, remind them of who they are in Christ and the great victory that can be theirs to the power of God living in them and through them. Give them grace and help them to process their failures at times, but speak to them of the wonderful power of God who enables us to overcome.

"Little children, keep yourselves from idols" (1 John 5:21). Lastly, John spoke to his children and exhorted them to keep themselves from idols. The tendency of the human heart to worship is strong within us. We will either worship God, which produces wonderful results in our lives, or we will worship self, success, relationships, intellect, sex, or a million other things. As your children grow older and older, help them navigate their hearts and show them the wonderful glory of God. They need to know from you how worthy He is of worship and adoration and sacrifice. He is the God who always gives back, unlike any idol ever worshipped by man.

Delight

For the Lord reproves him whom he loves, as a father the son in whom he delights. (Proverbs 3:12)

Yes, father, use your words well in the building up of your children throughout their young and precious lives. This will best occur if you simply delight in your children, as the proverb states (Proverbs 3:12). Give your time and your presence to your children. Spend yourself on them. To be a dad is such a wonderful privilege and honor. Give yourself fully to these little lives. Learn about them. Study them. As you give yourself to them, your delight in them will only grow. They will sense it and know it. They will be safe in your love.

Chapter 6

MAN

...the Man Christ Jesus... (1 Timothy 2:5)

In the midst of all of this, it is good for you to remember that you are a man. Yes, you are a son, a husband, a servant, a leader, and a dad, but you have a unique role in your family, that of a man. You might have *boys* growing up in your home, but you are the only *man* who lives under that roof. That said, you will perpetually be the readiest definition of manhood your entire family could draw upon. This doesn't mean you need to get all Rambo on them or anything. You don't need to start smoking a pipe, begin wearing chaps, or grow a *Duck Dynasty* beard to display your manliness. Just know that you are the man of the house, the one they look at to tell them what a man is all about.

Responsible

Fortunately, we have a strong model for what a man is all about in Jesus Christ the righteous. Jesus is the ultimate man. He wasn't Adventure Man, Hobby Man, or Obnoxiously Loud Man; he was the sacrificial Son of God who took our burdens and made them His own. This is, of course, a great definition of responsibility. Jesus, the ultimate man, took responsibility for us. He hadn't caused our problems or created our troubles, but *"He has borne our griefs and carried our sorrows"* (Isaiah 53:4). This wasn't His one-time act of service, however, as He continues to serve us from His position in heaven, since *"He always lives to make intercession for us"* (Hebrews 7:25). This man above all men became our great servant, responsible for us.

We live in a world screaming for young men to take responsibility. If you are young and a man, you are going to spend more for car insurance than any other demographic. That isn't arbitrary; there's a reason for it. In our video game-obsessed, pornography-addicted culture, there is a need for a generation of young men to rise up to take responsibility. But this is where we often fall short in our message. Responsibility isn't just "getting your act together," purchasing a calendar, and tucking in your shirt. No, Jesus took responsibility. He saw our weakness and our brokenness, and so completely owned it for us. He didn't leave us to fend for ourselves. The Man Christ Jesus stepped up and took responsibility for you.

God's men will be responsible for the lives entrusted into their care, including their own. They will sacrificially love and nurture their wives and children, leaving a legacy for generations. Perhaps your first child is on the way. Maybe you've already got little ones living in your house. Whatever the situation, be a man like Christ and take responsibility. Our flesh will scream at us to be self-serving, so this will be a continual battle, but Christ in us can strengthen us to lay our lives down for our loved ones.

Committed

Additionally, Jesus committed himself to us. His dedication and devotion chased Him all the way to the cross. It is been said that the nails did not hold Him to the cross, but that His extreme love and commitment to us held Him there. Jesus was all in. He was committed. He was always available to His disciples. He wasn't iffy about His mission. *"I have set my face like a flint, and I know that I shall not be put to shame"* (Isaiah 50:7). Unwaveringly, Jesus committed Himself to us.

In the same way, God's men, including young fathers, are called to be extremely committed men. Our families, especially our brides, ought to know of our deep and covenantal sense of calling to them. They experience security in our commitment. *"Like a bird that strays from its nest is a man who strays from his home"* (Proverbs 27:8). Don't stray. Don't wander. Throw yourself into your family. Sadly, many men begin to drift from their homes once children are introduced. Dirty diapers, a never-ending workload, and sleep deprivation freak them out. Life isn't like it was before. Their lack of commitment becomes glaring during these labor-intensive times. Be an unchanging rock of commitment to your family. Be around.

Jesus worked incredibly hard to serve His disciples. They were an endless task. Jesus *"Knew well the condition of His flocks, and gave attention to His herds"* (Proverbs 27:23). His work toward them was constant. He was committed.

I know firsthand how tiring the early years of a family can be. It can almost seem as if your identity has been swallowed up by your children. Still, give yourself to your home and family. Be present. And when you're present, be really present, fully engaged, actively involved. Look, you'll need the recliner or the garage from time to time, but your little ones need you and your time. Nothing can replace it. Be committed to them like Jesus is for you.

A Work in Progress

One glaring difference between us and Christ—and there are many—is that He is perfect and glorified, without fault or blemish. Fortunately, He is producing the same thing in us. When it comes to his position before God, a believer has been cleansed by the blood of Jesus and is as good as glorified in the sight of God. Oh, the wonderful grace of God! We are complete in Him! *"And those whom he predestined he also called, and those whom he called he also justified, and those whom he justified he also glorified"* (Romans 8:30). Additionally, however, God is practically sanctifying us, drawing the sin out of us, working in and on us. *"Now may the God of peace himself sanctify you completely, and may your whole spirit and soul and body be kept blameless at the coming of our Lord Jesus Christ"* (1 Thessalonians 5:23). He is faithful.

As a man, we are a work in progress. We aren't to strut around as if our children are the only ones called to grow up. No, with humility we receive the grace of God for change and transformation in our own lives. We also show our wives and children through our words as well as our actions how much we understand the Lord's desire to grow us and change us.

Here are four of those actions, actions that demonstrate our knowledge that we need to grow.

Through *accountability* to other men, continual *submission* to spiritual leadership in our lives, and the willingness to *sit under* the teaching of God's Word, we show our families our awareness of our deep need. *"Iron sharpens iron, and one man sharpens another,"* (Proverbs 27:17) so find good and godly men to be with on a regular basis, men who won't shrink from challenging you, men your wife would respect. Some men isolate themselves from other men, but *"Whoever isolates himself seeks his own desire; he breaks out against all sound judgment"* (Proverbs 18:1). Living on his little island of aloneness he convinces himself of his awesomeness and other's stupidity. Other guys surround themselves with fools, giving their families little hope that someone will speak wisdom into dad's life. If even a man as great as King David needed godly counselors and friends, so do we (see 1 Chronicles 27:25–33).

Confession of our sins, generally and specifically, to our wives and children will also give them hope that we are growing as men. It gives my daughters great delight when Daddy apologizes to them. They sense that I know how imperfect I am. It comforts them and releases me. Be an open book, especially with your bride. Living in the light kills the darkness. *"If we confess our sins, he is faithful and just to forgive us our sins and to cleanse us from all unrighteousness"* (1 John 1:9). Before David finally confessed his secret sin, adultery with Bathsheba and the subsequent murder of her husband, there was death in his bones. He declared, *"When I kept silent, my bones wasted away through my groaning all day long"* (Psalms 32:3). There were consequences for him, as there will be for us, but it brought life. Confess. Regularly. To the Lord. To the men in your life. To your wife. To your kids.

The *study of God's Word*, personally, corporately, and with the family will evidence our hunger for transformation. A man with a marked-up Bible and a full journal is likely a man who understands His need. I grew up in the home of a pastor, one who dedicated himself to the careful explanation of the Word of God to his congregation. While that didn't translate into some kind of supernatural transference of knowledge to me, his son, it did help. Perhaps you are brand new to the Bible and without a heritage like mine. Do your best. *"Do your best to present yourself to God as one approved, a worker who has no need to be ashamed, rightly handling the word of truth"* (2 Timothy 2:15). You have an entire life to get into His book. Get after it.

A life of prayer, demonstrated through thoughtful, reflective prayers, prayer lists, and solitary moments alone with God, will demonstrate a man who knows he is in need of power and strength beyond himself. Prayerlessness is really one of the chief evidences of our pride as it screams of independence, trusting our own devices. *"Humble yourselves, therefore, under the mighty hand of God so that at the proper time he may exalt you, casting all your anxieties on him, because he cares for you"* (1 Peter 5:6–7). Lay it all out before Him! He loves you. Cry out to Him.

Look, everyone in your life knows you are a work in progress; they just need to know that you know.

A Great Work

I am doing a great work and I cannot come down. Why should the work stop while I leave it? (Nehemiah 6:3)

You and I are called to a great and incredible work. The building of love of family and the raising of a child are incomparably exciting endeavors. Should God in His grace and providence allow you to father a child, rejoice! This is the opportunity of a lifetime. No matter what your past has looked like, your future, because of Christ, can be so bright.

I know many young men who are embarking on this great journey. Many of them love the Lord and have apprehension and a little bit of fear coursing through their veins. That healthy respect of the role they are stepping into is a good thing. God will use them. God can use you as well.

You can do this. As Paul told Timothy, *"The Lord stood by me and strengthened me,"* and He will also strengthen you (2 Timothy 4:17).

A PRAYER

Father, thank You for Your great grace and mercy upon our lives. Thank You for Your wonderful love toward us and the beautiful opportunity to raise children for You.

I pray, Father, that our children would grow up to be like arrows in the hands of a warrior, shot out into this world by You.

Father, please equip and empower every man who reads this book. Strengthen us to be remarkable blessings to our wives, children, and world. Expand and grow Your kingdom and Your fame and Your glory, through our lives.

In moments, Father, when we are in need of wisdom, particularly at crossroads in the lives of our children, times when we need divine guidance, please speak to our hearts. Show us the way in which we should go.

Father, keep us from temptation and deliver us from evil. Defend these men from life-dominating sin and addictions or secret crimes of the flesh that would hinder their fatherly role.

Watch over us. Deepen us. Strengthen us. Use these men for Your honor and glory. Use their children.

Thank You, Father. In Jesus's name, Amen.

About the Author

Pastor Nate Holdridge loves Jesus and the Bible Jesus gave to the world. Since 1996, the Scripture has captivated Nate's mind and heart, believing the entirety of the book points to the Son of God, Jesus Christ the righteous (Revelation 19:10, John 5:36).

Having grown up in the home of a pastor, at age 18, Nate began to sense a strong desire to communicate Scripture with whomever God would allow him to speak to, and he has committed himself to that responsibility ever since. As the lead pastor of Calvary Monterey, Nate loves and enjoys the privilege of publicly reading, explaining, and exhorting from God's Word. In 2013 Nate set about the process of teaching from Genesis through Revelation in a series of studio recorded messages designed to edify and ground the body of Christ, having himself grown immensely from the recorded through-the-Bible teaching ministries of pastors such as Chuck Smith, Jon Courson, Joe Focht, Sandy Adams, Skip Heitzig, Brian Broderson, David Guzik, and his own father, Bill Holdridge, to name a few.

Nate loves being a husband and father, and has been happily married to his beautiful wife, Christina, since 2002. Together they live in Monterey, California, raising and enjoying their three amazing daughters and leading within their local church. A graduate of Calvary Chapel Bible College, Nate commits his time and energy to teaching Scripture and leading Calvary Monterey, and is especially interested in the development of godly men. Nate hopes you enjoy any and every resource you might utilize here, and is especially grateful for any and every opportunity Jesus gives him to serve His church.

For more information on Nate Holdridge visit nateholdridge.com.

Made in the USA
San Bernardino, CA
20 May 2015